BUILD YOUR OWN
FIGHTER PLANES

Norman Schmidt

STERLING INNOVATION
An imprint of Sterling Publishing Co., Inc.

New York / London
www.sterlingpublishing.com

STERLING, the Sterling logo, STERLING INNOVATION, and the Sterling Innovation logo are registered trademarks of Sterling Publishing Co., Inc.

2 4 6 8 10 9 7 5 3

Published by Sterling Publishing Co., Inc.
387 Park Avenue South, New York, NY 10016
© 2009 Norman Schmidt

This book is comprised of materials from the
following Sterling Publishing Co., Inc. / Tamos title:
Great Paper Fighter Planes © 2004 Norman Schmidt

Distributed in Canada by Sterling Publishing
c/o Canadian Manda Group, 165 Dufferin Street
Toronto, Ontario, Canada M6K 3H6
Distributed in the United Kingdom by GMC Distribution Services
Castle Place, 166 High Street, Lewes, East Sussex, England BN7 1XU
Distributed in Australia by Capricorn Link (Australia) Pty. Ltd.
P.O. Box 704, Windsor, NSW 2756, Australia

This book is part of the *Build Your Own Fighter Planes* book and kit
and is not to be sold separately.

Sterling ISBN 978-1-4027-6746-3

For information about custom editions, special sales, premium and
corporate purchases, please contact Sterling Special Sales
Department at 800-805-5489 or specialsales@sterlingpublishing.com.

CONTENTS

INTRODUCTION

For those who enjoy making things, paper airplanes are a fun way to learn about aviation and how airplanes fly. Through representative examples from the hundreds of types of fighter planes built by various countries, the models and accompanying text in this book outline the progress in airplane design through the years.

Paper models that are cut from standard index card and constructed with care, have reasonable flight characteristics. With details added they become convincing representations of the real thing.

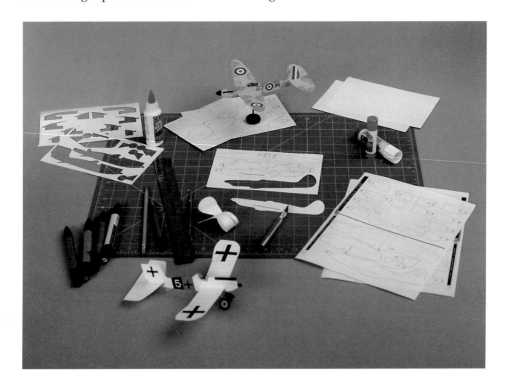

In the models shown, only enough detail is included to place each model in the right era, with no attempt made to accurately represent the markings of any air force or squadron. (Including the many thousands of different markings used in military aircraft is beyond the scope of this book. If accuracy in the markings is important, these may be found in books on the subject and on the Internet.)

The proportions of the models are altered somewhat from their full-sized counterparts to suit the paper medium, and they are not in scale with each other. Notice in particular that the tails are large in relation to the rest of the plane. This is necessary to improve flight performance in such small-scale models.

Besides building and decorating the paper planes, all kinds of additional fun activities are possible by having flight competitions. These might include straight distance flights, landing as close as possible to some particular spot, flying through a hoop, or stunt flights.

GENERAL INSTRUCTIONS

Begin by reading and studying all the instruction pages and practicing the basic techniques.

Always work on a large flat surface so you can spread things out. Make sure there is plenty of light so you can see what you are doing. If you have never made anything from paper, or have never used a craft knife, you should begin with some practice. In pencil, draw some squares, triangles, and circles of various sizes on index card stock and cut them out. Use a sharp craft knife (e.g. an X-ACTO knife with a #11 blade) on a suitable cutting surface (e.g. an Olfa cutting mat). Practice cutting precisely on the line. Always keep the blade sharp, and cut by drawing the knife towards you—away from the hand used to hold the paper.

Scoring a fold line can be done by using a ballpoint pen that has run dry. The indentation left by this tool makes for more accurate folding. To make straight cuts and score lines, use a steel-edged ruler to guide the tools. Make freehand cuts and scores for curved lines. Continue to practice until you are comfortable with the tools.

TO BUILD A MODEL

First build less complicated models, such as the Yak-18. Once simpler models have been mastered, move on to the complicated ones, such as the biplanes.

STEP 1
Prepare parts for cutting
This kit offers two ways to create models:
1. Look over the 5 x 8-inch cards included in the kit. These will make a one-time model. The stock of paper is perfect for model airplanes, and every part needed to make each plane in the book can be found on the cards.
2. Make same-sized photocopies (100%) of the template pages containing the parts for building the paper models. Each photocopied page contains 2 sections. Cut them apart. The parts for each model occupy either 3 or 4 sections. Each section fits a standard 5 x 8-inch index card. Tack-glue each photocopied section to an index card by applying glue to the backside and aligning it with the edges of the card. For this, use low-tack glue (e.g. Elmer's Office Self Stick Notes glue. If regular glue is used, be sure to glue between the parts only.)

Save the template pages so you can create these models again and again. The more you make them, the better they will be.

STEP 2
Advanced planning
Before beginning to cut out the parts, score those parts that will need to be bent later (shown as dotted lines). Then cut opening slits in fuselage parts (shown as dashed lines). Score and cut precisely on the lines.

STEP 3
Cut out the parts
Cut out each part shown. This must be done carefully, since the success or failure of every other step depends on accurately made parts.

Discard the excess paper. This leaves a clean, unmarked airplane part ready for assembly. Keep track of the parts by lightly writing the part number in pencil on the backside of each part.

For all the cut-out pieces, the side that faces up for cutting will be outward or upward facing on the finished plane. This is important for aerodynamic and aesthetic reasons.

STEP 4
Build the fuselage

Follow the sequence shown in the assembly diagrams (an exploded view) given for each model. Begin with the number 1 fuselage part, adding the other smaller parts on each side to complete the fuselage. Note which is the front of each part (marked with a small arrow). Align parts carefully. Take care to position the bent-over parts accurately because they are the fastening tabs for wings and horizontal stabilizer.

Use a glue stick (e.g. Uhu Color Glue Stic), white craft glue, or wood-type model airplane glue when assembling the parts. Note, it is easier to manage the drying time and reduce warpage with stick glue.

When building up the main parts in layers, apply glue to the entire smaller piece that is to be fastened to a larger one. Press parts firmly together. Continue until the entire main part is completed.

Lay the assembled fuselage flat between clean sheets of paper underneath a weight (some heavy books) until the glue is sufficiently set. This will take between 30 and 45 minutes for stick glue, and longer for white glue. When dry, the glue acts as a stiffener for the model.

STEP 5
Build the wings

Symmetry is essential for wings. Special care must be taken in the wings of biplanes. Make sure that the struts are carefully positioned at the points indicated so that upper and lower wings align at the leading (front) edges.

The dihedral angle (upward slanting of wings from center to tips) must be adjusted while the parts are being assembled, before the glue is set. (Consult the angle guide given with each model.) If stick glue is used, simply prop up the wings at the tips until the glue has set. If white glue or model glue is used, drying the wings is more complicated. Some means must be devised to keep each wing from warping while maintaining the dihedral angle.

STEP 6
Adding details
The time to add decoration and color—such as numbers, insignia, and camouflage—is when the glue is dry but before the model is assembled. For this, use colored pencils and/or non-toxic felt-tipped markers. Add as much or as little detail as you wish.

STEP 7
Put it all together
To assemble the model, apply white glue to the bent-over tabs that join the wings and horizontal stabilizer to the fuselage. Align the wings and stabilizers carefully. Press glued parts together. For those models with a fixed undercarriage, use white glue to fasten wheels where indicated. Adjust placement of parts carefully, viewing the plane from the top, the front, and the back. Symmetry and straightness in the completed plane are essential. Allow plenty of time for glue to dry.

STEP 8
Wing camber and washout

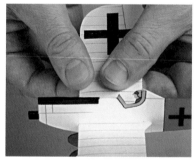

This is a critical step. Cambering the wings gives them their ability to generate aerodynamic lift. Washout aids in flight stability. For washout, gently twist each wing until the trailing edge at the wingtip is higher than at the root. For camber, hold a wing at the root between thumb and forefinger of both hands. Gently massage the paper to give the upper surface a slight convex curvature or camber (bottom

To camber a wing, gently massage the paper to give the upper surface a convex curvature.

becomes concave). Work carefully from the wing root toward the tip and back again. The point of maximum camber should lie about one third of the way back from the front edge of the wing. Make sure that the left and right wings have the same amount of camber and washout. Avoid kinking the paper.

STEP 9

Flying, displaying, storing

Paper models must be well trimmed (adjusted) before they can perform satisfactorily. Ensure that the plane is not bent or twisted in any way. When properly handled and stored, these models can last a long time.

TIPS

Handling paper models

Pick up and hold paper airplanes by the nose, their sturdiest part. Never lift them by the wings or tail; this will distort their aerodynamic shape.

Preflight inspection

After a paper plane is finished and the glue is completely dried, do a preflight inspection and make any necessary adjustments.

Examine the plane thoroughly from the front, back, top, bottom, and sides. Check for parts that appear bent or twisted. Correct any defects by gently massaging the paper to work out bends and twists. A paper airplane must be symmetrical, with each side exactly like the other in terms of shape, size, camber, dihedral, and wing washout.

Test flights

The objective of test flights is to trim (adjust) the model for straight and level flight at its best speed. Try to test fly in calm conditions so that each flight is more predictable.

Hold the fuselage between thumb and forefinger just behind the plane's center of gravity. Throw it gently with a straight-ahead motion.

To correct a dive, the elevator needs adjusting by bending it up slightly to give positive trim.

If a paper plane banks and turns in either direction, it is always due to one wing producing more lift than the other. First, make sure that the camber is identical in both wings. If camber is slightly greater in one wing, the plane will bank and turn in the opposite direction. Second, make sure that the wings have a slight, equal washout and generate equal lift. The wingtip that is lower at the trailing edge will cause the wing to lift and the plane to bank and turn in the opposite direction.

A slightly bent fuselage will also cause the plane to turn by yawing left or right. Make the fuselage as straight as possible. For a final correction, adjust the rudder by bending it in the opposite direction to the turn.

If the plane climbs, loses speed, and pitches down sharply (stalls), the elevator needs to be bent down slightly. However, if this problem cannot be corrected without the elevator being bent down below the straight level, the airplane's center of gravity is too far back and additional ballast is needed in the nose. Glue additional layers of paper onto the nose.

Extending the flight

Launch the paper plane across the wind, letting it turn downwind gradually. The wind speed will add to actual airspeed, increasing the ability to cover distance over the ground. Launching across the wind reduces the chances that the plane will stall from a steep climb, which can happen when it's launched into the wind, or from decreased relative airspeed—common in downwind launches.

Another way to fly a paper plane is to begin the flight with a high launch. The plane's control surfaces should be trimmed for a gentle left or right turn. (If the pilot is right-handed, trim for a gentle turn to the left.) Make these trim adjustments in very slight increments until the desired turn rate is achieved.

Launch the plane in an inclined position with considerable force upward and away from your body (about 45 degrees), across the wind. It gains altitude from the force of the throw, but loses speed as it climbs. The plane may also make a complete loop and gain equilibrium. Because of the altitude gained by the high launch, the descent should be a good long flight.

Paper is a relatively unstable material, so it may be necessary to readjust the planes after every few flights.

Storing the models

When carefully handled, these paper planes can last a long time. To keep them from becoming damaged or warped when not in use, they need proper storage. One way is to hang them by the nose from a line using clothespins.

A handy portable storage "hangar" can be made by stringing the line inside a large cardboard box.

Wheels

Planes from World War I all have fixed nonretracting undercarriages. The paper models are designed to fly with these in place. One way to display these planes is to simply set them on their wheels.

Planes from World War II and later have retracting undercarriages, and these planes are designed to fly without main wheels attached. However, the models can be built with them attached for display purposes, if desired.

The paper pieces to make the wheels of all models are included on the parts layout pages. Attachment points are indicated with gray lines.

Suspended

Another way to display paper models is to suspend them by threads attached to their fuselages at the center of gravity.

#1 FOKKER E.I EINDECKER

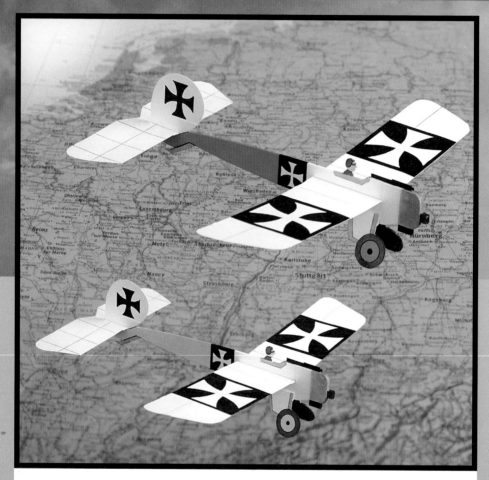

Year: 1915
Country of origin: Germany
Manufacturer: Fokker Flugzeug-Werke
Type: Single-seat fighter
Engine: 100 hp Oberursel 9-cylinder air
cooled rotary
Wingspan: approx 31 ft (9 m)

Length: approx 23 ft (7 m)
Height: approx 9 ft 10in (3 m)
Weight: 1,342 1b (610kg)
Maximum speed: 88 mph
Service ceiling: 11,500 ft (3,500m)
Range: 113 miles (182 km)
Armament: One machine gun

Note: Given the fact that fighter design evolved rapidly in the 20th century, specifications for each fighter type varied considerably depending on exactly when and where it was produced. What is given in this book are generalizations.

ASSEMBLY

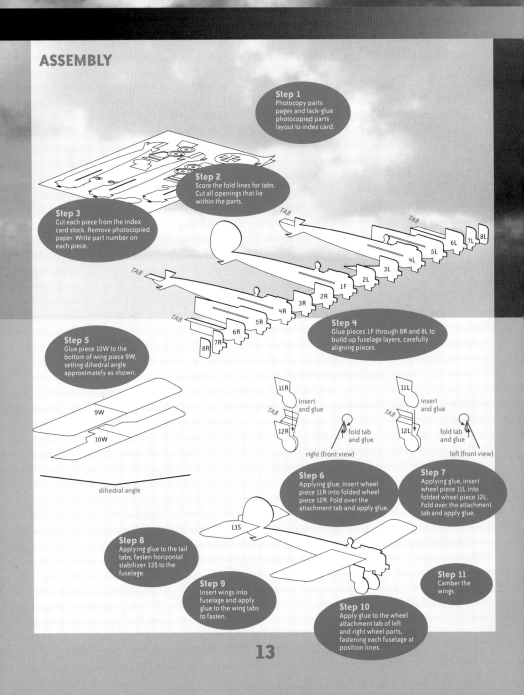

Step 1
Photocopy parts pages and tack-glue photocopied parts layout to index card.

Step 2
Score the fold lines for tabs. Cut all openings that lie within the parts.

Step 3
Cut each piece from the index card stock. Remove photocopied paper. Write part number on each piece.

Step 4
Glue pieces 1F through 8R and 8L to build up fuselage layers, carefully aligning pieces.

Step 5
Glue piece 10W to the bottom of wing piece 9W, setting dihedral angle approximately as shown.

Step 6
Applying glue, insert wheel piece 11R into folded wheel piece 12R. Fold over the attachment tab and apply glue.

Step 7
Applying glue, insert wheel piece 11L into folded wheel piece 12L. Fold over the attachment tab and apply glue.

Step 8
Applying glue to the tail tabs, fasten horizontal stabilizer 13S to the fuselage.

Step 9
Insert wings into fuselage and apply glue to the wing tabs to fasten.

Step 10
Apply glue to the wheel attachment tab of left and right wheel parts, fastening each fuselage at position lines.

Step 11
Camber the wings.

13

#2 NIEUPORT 17

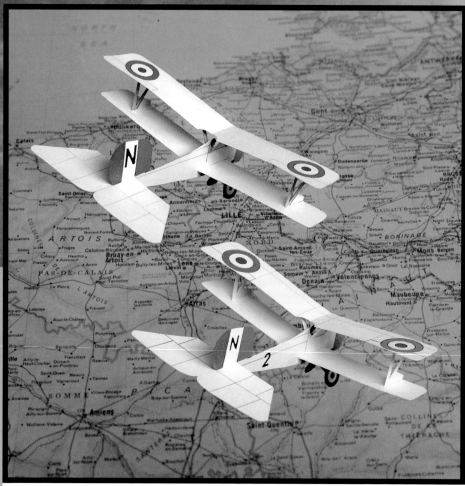

Year: 1916
Country of origin: France
Type: Single-seat fighter
Engine: Le Rhône 9J, 9-cylinder, rotary, 110 hp
Wingspan: 26 ft 11 in (8.22 m)
Length: 18 ft 10 in (5.74 m)

Height: 7 ft 10 in
Weight: 1,246 lb (565 kg)
Maximum speed: 110 mph (177 km/h)
Service ceiling: 17,388 ft (5,300 m)
Endurance: 2 hours
Armament: One Lewis machine gun

ASSEMBLY

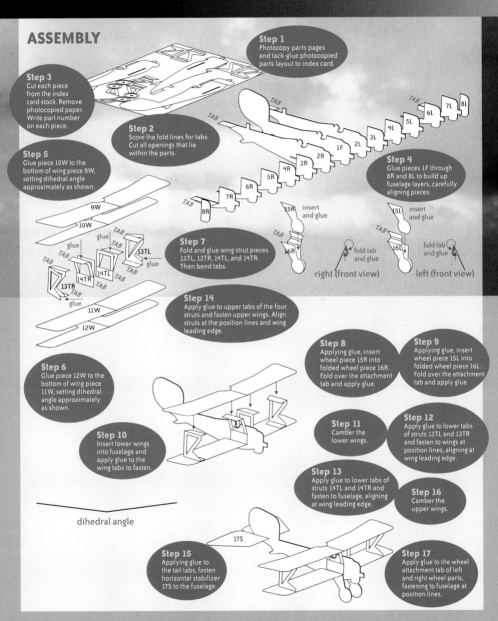

Step 1
Photocopy parts pages and tack-glue photocopied parts layout to index card.

Step 3
Cut each piece from the index card stock. Remove photocopied paper. Write part number on each piece.

Step 2
Score the fold lines for tabs. Cut all openings that lie within the parts.

Step 4
Glue pieces 1F through 8R and 8L to build up fuselage layers, carefully aligning pieces.

Step 5
Glue piece 10W to the bottom of wing piece 9W, setting dihedral angle approximately as shown.

Step 7
Fold and glue wing strut pieces 13TL, 13TR, 14TL, and 14TR. Then bend tabs.

insert and glue — right (front view)

insert and glue — left (front view)

fold tab and glue

Step 14
Apply glue to upper tabs of the four struts and fasten upper wings. Align struts at the position lines and wing leading edge.

Step 6
Glue piece 12W to the bottom of wing piece 11W, setting dihedral angle approximately as shown.

Step 8
Applying glue, insert wheel piece 15R into folded wheel piece 16R. Fold over the attachment tab and apply glue.

Step 9
Applying glue, insert wheel piece 15L into folded wheel piece 16L. Fold over the attachment tab and apply glue.

Step 10
Insert lower wings into fuselage and apply glue to the wing tabs to fasten.

Step 11
Camber the lower wings.

Step 12
Apply glue to lower tabs of struts 13TL and 13TR and fasten to wings at position lines, aligning at wing leading edge.

Step 13
Apply glue to lower tabs of struts 14TL and 14TR and fasten to fuselage, aligning at wing leading edge.

Step 16
Camber the upper wings.

dihedral angle

Step 15
Applying glue to the tail tabs, fasten horizontal stabilizer 17S to the fuselage.

Step 17
Apply glue to the wheel attachment tab of left and right wheel parts, fastening to fuselage at position lines.

15

#3 ALBATROS D.III

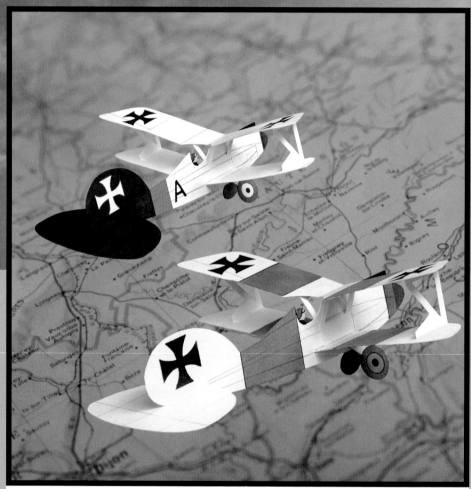

Year: 1917
Country of origin: Germany
Manufacturer: Albatros Werke
Type: Single-seat fighter
Engine: Mercedes 160 hp inline liquid cooled
Wingspan: 29 ft 7 in (9 m)

Length: 24 ft (7.3 m)
Height: 9 ft 4 in (2.8 m)
Maximum speed: 116 mph (186 km/h)
Service ceiling: 18,700 ft (5,610 m)
Range: 300 miles (480 km)
Armament: Two Spandau machine guns

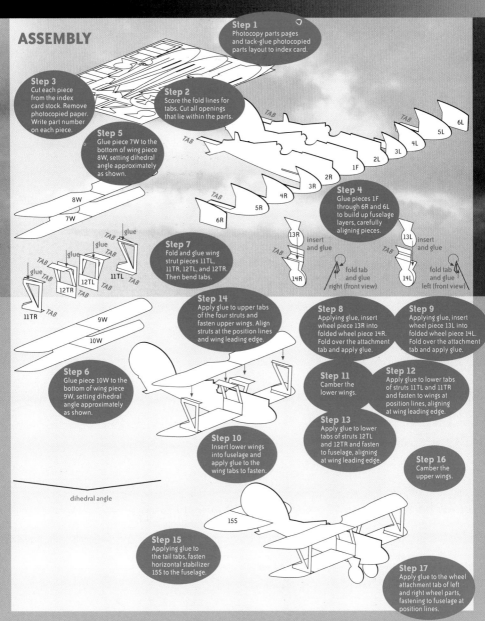

ASSEMBLY

Step 1
Photocopy parts pages and tack-glue photocopied parts layout to index card.

Step 2
Score the fold lines for tabs. Cut all openings that lie within the parts.

Step 3
Cut each piece from the index card stock. Remove photocopied paper. Write part number on each piece.

Step 4
Glue pieces 1F through 6R and 6L to build up fuselage layers, carefully aligning pieces.

Step 5
Glue piece 7W to the bottom of wing piece 8W, setting dihedral angle approximately as shown.

Step 6
Glue piece 10W to the bottom of wing piece 9W, setting dihedral angle approximately as shown.

Step 7
Fold and glue wing strut pieces 11TL, 11TR, 12TL, and 12TR. Then bend tabs.

Step 8
Applying glue, insert wheel piece 13R into folded wheel piece 14R. Fold over the attachment tab and apply glue.

Step 9
Applying glue, insert wheel piece 13L into folded wheel piece 14L. Fold over the attachment tab and apply glue.

Step 10
Insert lower wings into fuselage and apply glue to the wing tabs to fasten.

Step 11
Camber the lower wings.

Step 12
Apply glue to lower tabs of struts 11TL and 11TR and fasten to wings at position lines, aligning at wing leading edge.

Step 13
Apply glue to lower tabs of struts 12TL and 12TR and fasten to fuselage, aligning at wing leading edge.

Step 14
Apply glue to upper tabs of the four struts and fasten upper wings. Align struts at the position lines and wing leading edge.

Step 15
Applying glue to the tail tabs, fasten horizontal stabilizer 15S to the fuselage.

Step 16
Camber the upper wings.

Step 17
Apply glue to the wheel attachment tab of left and right wheel parts, fastening to fuselage at position lines.

17

#4 SOPWITH CAMEL

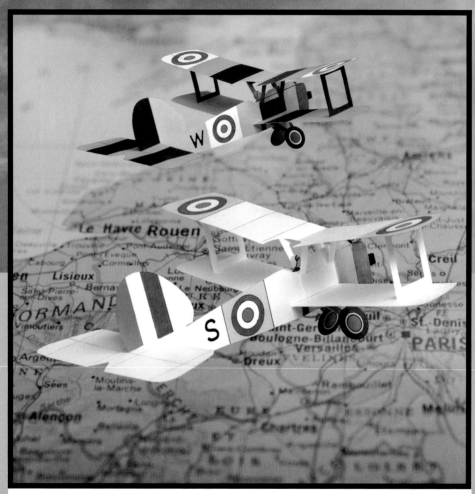

Year: 1917
Country of origin: Great Britain
Manufacturer: Sopwith
Type: Single-seat fighter
Engine: Bentley BR-1 150 hp air cooled rotary
Wingspan: 28 ft (8.4 m)

Length: 18 ft 8 in (5.1 m)
Height: 8 ft 6 in (2.5 m)
Maximum speed: 118 mph (189 km/h)
Service ceiling: 19,000 ft. (5,700 m)
Endurance: 2.5 hrs
Armament: Two Vickers .303 machine guns

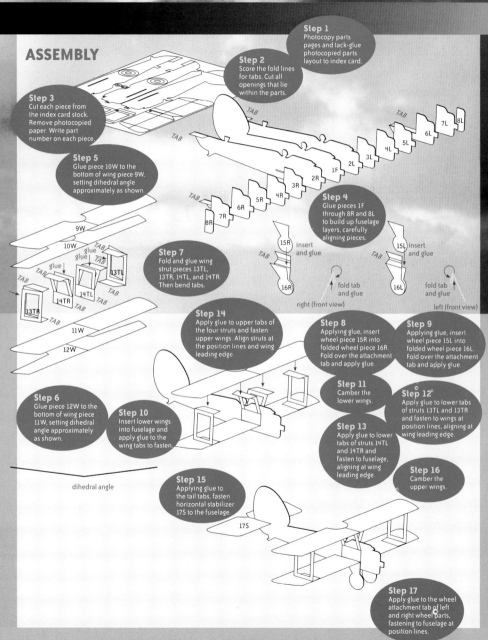

ASSEMBLY

Step 1
Photocopy parts pages and tack-glue photocopied parts layout to index card.

Step 2
Score the fold lines for tabs. Cut all openings that lie within the parts.

Step 3
Cut each piece from the index card stock. Remove photocopied paper. Write part number on each piece.

Step 4
Glue pieces 1F through 8R and 8L to build up fuselage layers, carefully aligning pieces.

Step 5
Glue piece 10W to the bottom of wing piece 9W, setting dihedral angle approximately as shown.

Step 6
Glue piece 12W to the bottom of wing piece 11W, setting dihedral angle approximately as shown.

Step 7
Fold and glue wing strut pieces 13TL, 13TR, 14TL, and 14TR. Then bend tabs.

Step 8
Applying glue, insert wheel piece 15R into folded wheel piece 16R. Fold over the attachment tab and apply glue.

Step 9
Applying glue, insert wheel piece 15L into folded wheel piece 16L. Fold over the attachment tab and apply glue.

Step 10
Insert lower wings into fuselage and apply glue to the wing tabs to fasten.

Step 11
Camber the lower wings.

Step 12
Apply glue to lower tabs of struts 13TL and 13TR and fasten to wings at position lines, aligning at wing leading edge.

Step 13
Apply glue to lower tabs of struts 14TL and 14TR and fasten to fuselage, aligning at wing leading edge.

Step 14
Apply glue to upper tabs of the four struts and fasten upper wings. Align struts at the position lines and wing leading edge.

Step 15
Applying glue to the tail tabs, fasten horizontal stabilizer 17S to the fuselage.

Step 16
Camber the upper wings.

Step 17
Apply glue to the wheel attachment tab of left and right wheel parts, fastening to fuselage at position lines.

insert and glue — fold tab and glue — right (front view)

insert and glue — fold tab and glue — left (front view)

dihedral angle

#5 SPAD XIII

Year: 1917
Country of origin: France
Manufacturer: Societe pour Aviation et ses Derives
Type: Single-seat fighter
Engine: Hispano-Suiza 150 hp liquid cooled
Wingspan: 25 ft 6 in (7.7 m)

Length: 20 ft 1 in (6.1 m)
Height: 7 ft (2.1 m)
Maximum speed: 119 mph (192 km/h)
Service ceiling: 18,000 ft (5,485 m)
Range: 185 miles (298 km)
Armament: Two Vickers machine guns

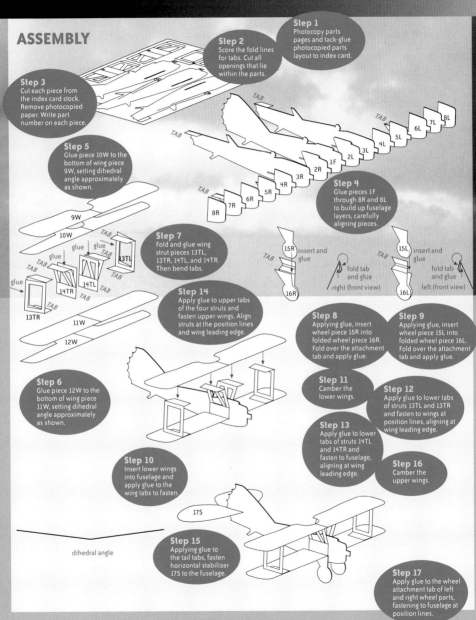

ASSEMBLY

Step 1
Photocopy parts pages and tack-glue photocopied parts layout to index card.

Step 2
Score the fold lines for tabs. Cut all openings that lie within the parts.

Step 3
Cut each piece from the index card stock. Remove photocopied paper. Write part number on each piece.

Step 5
Glue piece 10W to the bottom of wing piece 9W, setting dihedral angle approximately as shown.

Step 4
Glue pieces 1F through 8R and 8L to build up fuselage layers, carefully aligning pieces.

Step 7
Fold and glue wing strut pieces 13TL, 13TR, 14TL, and 14TR. Then bend tabs.

Step 8
Applying glue, insert wheel piece 15R into folded wheel piece 16R. Fold over the attachment tab and apply glue.

Step 9
Applying glue, insert wheel piece 15L into folded wheel piece 16L. Fold over the attachment tab and apply glue.

Step 14
Apply glue to upper tabs of the four struts and fasten upper wings. Align struts at the position lines and wing leading edge.

Step 6
Glue piece 12W to the bottom of wing piece 11W, setting dihedral angle approximately as shown.

Step 11
Camber the lower wings.

Step 12
Apply glue to lower tabs of struts 13TL and 13TR and fasten to wings at position lines, aligning at wing leading edge.

Step 13
Apply glue to lower tabs of struts 14TL and 14TR and fasten to fuselage, aligning at wing leading edge.

Step 16
Camber the upper wings.

Step 10
Insert lower wings into fuselage and apply glue to the wing tabs to fasten.

Step 15
Applying glue to the tail tabs, fasten horizontal stabilizer 17S to the fuselage.

Step 17
Apply glue to the wheel attachment tab of left and right wheel parts, fastening to fuselage at position lines.

#6 JUNKERS D.I

Year: 1918
Country of origin: Germany
Manufacturer: Junkers
Type: Single-seat fighter
Engine: Mercedes 180 hp liquid cooled
Wingspan: 29 ft 6 in (8.9 m)

Length: 23 ft 9 in (7.2 m)
Height: 7 ft 4 in (2.2 m)
Maximum speed: 118 mph (189 km/h)
Service ceiling: 18,000 ft (5,485 m)
Armament: Two Spandau machine guns

ASSEMBLY

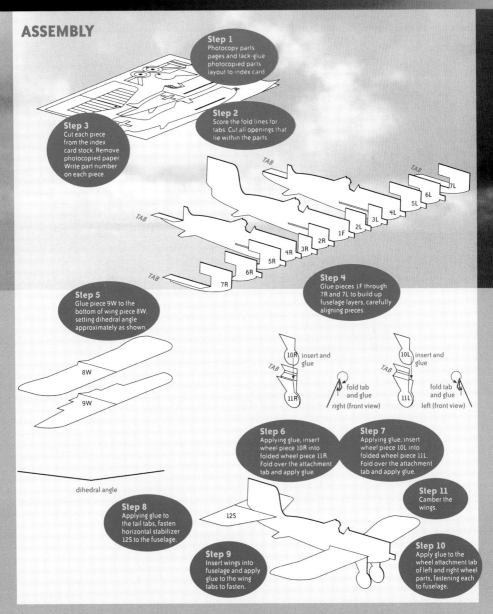

Step 1
Photocopy parts pages and tack-glue photocopied parts layout to index card.

Step 2
Score the fold lines for tabs. Cut all openings that lie within the parts.

Step 3
Cut each piece from the index card stock. Remove photocopied paper. Write part number on each piece.

Step 4
Glue pieces 1F through 7R and 7L to build up fuselage layers, carefully aligning pieces.

Step 5
Glue piece 9W to the bottom of wing piece 8W, setting dihedral angle approximately as shown.

dihedral angle

10R insert and glue
TAB
11R
fold tab and glue
right (front view)

10L insert and glue
TAB
11L
fold tab and glue
left (front view)

Step 6
Applying glue, insert wheel piece 10R into folded wheel piece 11R. Fold over the attachment tab and apply glue.

Step 7
Applying glue, insert wheel piece 10L into folded wheel piece 11L. Fold over the attachment tab and apply glue.

Step 11
Camber the wings.

Step 8
Applying glue to the tail tabs, fasten horizontal stabilizer 12S to the fuselage.

Step 9
Insert wings into fuselage and apply glue to the wing tabs to fasten.

Step 10
Apply glue to the wheel attachment tab of left and right wheel parts, fastening each to fuselage.

#7 MESSERSCHMITT BF 109

Year: 1935
Country of origin: Germany
Manufacturer: Messerschmitt
Type: Single-seat fighter/fighter-bomber
Engine: One 1,400 hp Daimler-Benz, inline,
liquid cooled, supercharger
Wingspan: 32 ft 7 in (9.9 m)

Length: 29 ft 7 in (9 m)
Height: 11 ft 2 in (3.4 m)
Maximum speed: 386 mph (623 km/h)
Service ceiling: 38,500 ft (11,750 m)
Range: 450 miles (725 km)
Armament: Two cowl-mounted 7.92 mm
machine guns, one hub-firing 30 mm cannon,
two wing-mounted 20 mm cannon

ASSEMBLY

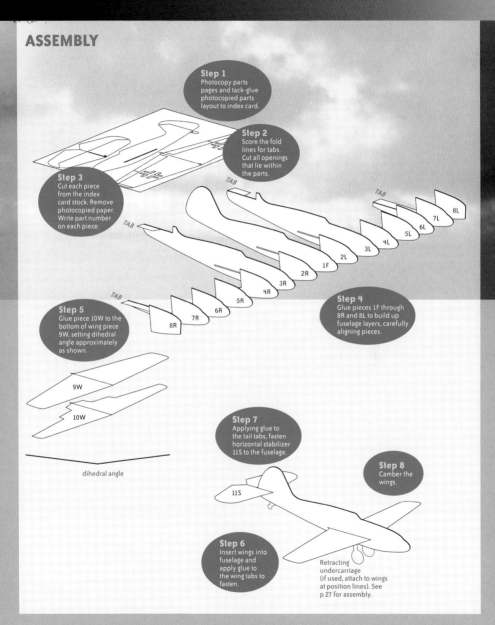

Step 1
Photocopy parts pages and tack-glue photocopied parts layout to index card.

Step 2
Score the fold lines for tabs. Cut all openings that lie within the parts.

Step 3
Cut each piece from the index card stock. Remove photocopied paper. Write part number on each piece.

Step 4
Glue pieces 1F through 8R and 8L to build up fuselage layers, carefully aligning pieces.

Step 5
Glue piece 10W to the bottom of wing piece 9W, setting dihedral angle approximately as shown.

Step 6
Insert wings into fuselage and apply glue to the wing tabs to fasten.

Step 7
Applying glue to the tail tabs, fasten horizontal stabilizer 11S to the fuselage.

Step 8
Camber the wings.

TAB

TAB

TAB

TAB

8L
7L
6L
5L
4L
3L
2L
1F
2R
3R
4R
5R
6R
7R
8R

9W
10W

dihedral angle

11S

Retracting undercarriage (if used, attach to wings at position lines). See p 27 for assembly.

25

#8 CURTISS P-40 WARHAWK

Year: 1938
Country of origin: United States of America
Manufacturer: Curtiss
Type: Single-seat fighter/fighter-bomber
Engine: One 1,160 hp Allison, 12-cylinder, Vee, liquid cooled, supercharger
Wingspan: 37 ft 4 in (11.4 m)

Length: 33 ft 4 in (10.2 m)
Height: 12 ft 4 in (3.8 m)
Maximum speed: 343 mph (552 km/h)
Service ceiling: 30,000 ft (9,144 m)
Range: 750 miles (1,207 km)
Armament: Six 0.5 in Browning machine guns, three external 500 lb bombs

ASSEMBLY

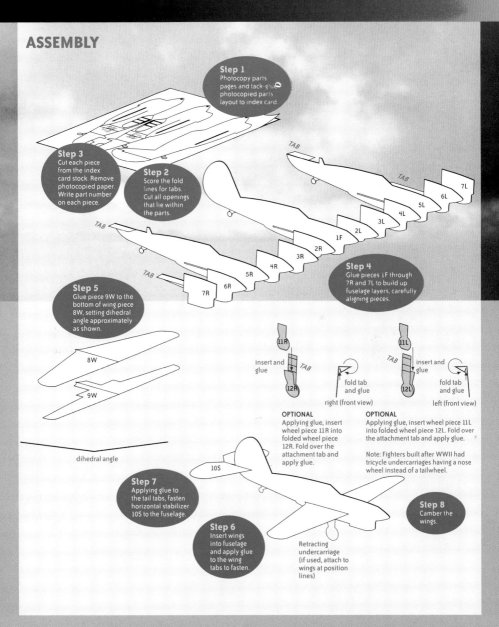

Step 1
Photocopy parts pages and tack-glue photocopied parts layout to index card.

Step 3
Cut each piece from the index card stock. Remove photocopied paper. Write part number on each piece.

Step 2
Score the fold lines for tabs. Cut all openings that lie within the parts.

Step 4
Glue pieces 1F through 7R and 7L to build up fuselage layers, carefully aligning pieces.

Step 5
Glue piece 9W to the bottom of wing piece 8W, setting dihedral angle approximately as shown.

dihedral angle

insert and glue

fold tab and glue

right (front view)

TAB

insert and glue

fold tab and glue

left (front view)

OPTIONAL
Applying glue, insert wheel piece 11R into folded wheel piece 12R. Fold over the attachment tab and apply glue.

OPTIONAL
Applying glue, insert wheel piece 11L into folded wheel piece 12L. Fold over the attachment tab and apply glue.

Note: Fighters built after WWII had tricycle undercarriages having a nose wheel instead of a tailwheel.

Step 7
Applying glue to the tail tabs, fasten horizontal stabilizer 10S to the fuselage.

Step 6
Insert wings into fuselage and apply glue to the wing tabs to fasten.

Retracting undercarriage (if used, attach to wings at position lines)

Step 8
Camber the wings.

#9 SUPERMARINE SPITFIRE

Year: 1938
Country of origin: Great Britain
Manufacturer: Supermarine
Type: Single-seat fighter/fighter-bomber
Engine: One 1,440 hp Rolls-Royce Merlin,
12-cylinder, Vee, liquid cooled, supercharger
Wingspan: 36 ft 10 in (11.2 m)

Length: 29 ft 11 in (9.1 m)
Height: 11 ft 5 in (3.5 m)
Maximum speed: 374 mph (602 km/h)
Service ceiling: 37,000 ft (11,280 m)
Range: 470 miles (756 km)
Armament: Two 20 mm cannon and four .303
machine guns in the wings or no cannon and
eight machine guns

ASSEMBLY

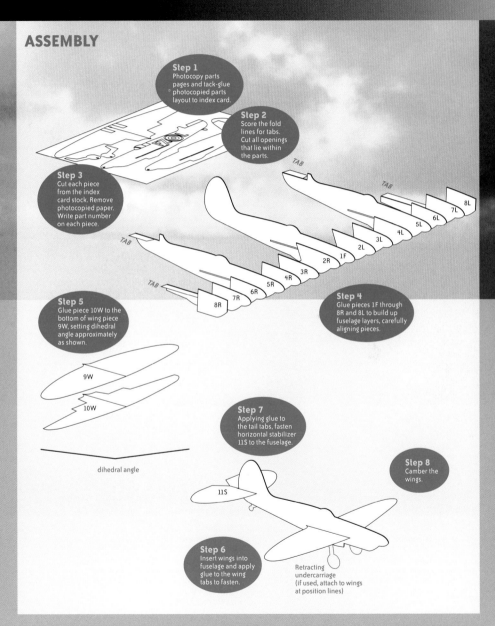

Step 1
Photocopy parts pages and tack-glue photocopied parts layout to index card.

Step 2
Score the fold lines for tabs. Cut all openings that lie within the parts.

Step 3
Cut each piece from the index card stock. Remove photocopied paper. Write part number on each piece.

Step 4
Glue pieces 1F through 8R and 8L to build up fuselage layers, carefully aligning pieces.

Step 5
Glue piece 10W to the bottom of wing piece 9W, setting dihedral angle approximately as shown.

Step 6
Insert wings into fuselage and apply glue to the wing tabs to fasten.

Step 7
Applying glue to the tail tabs, fasten horizontal stabilizer 11S to the fuselage.

Step 8
Camber the wings.

dihedral angle

Retracting undercarriage (if used, attach to wings at position lines)

#10 MITSUBISHI A6M ZERO

Year: 1940
Country of origin: Japan
Manufacturer: Mitsubishi
Type: Single-seat fighter/fighter-bomber
Engine: One 1,100 hp Nakajima air-cooled radial, supercharger
Wingspan: 36 ft 1 in (11 m)

Length: 29 ft 11 in (9.1 m)
Height: 11 ft 6 in (3.5 m)
Maximum speed: 351 mph (565 km/h)
Service ceiling: 38,500 ft (11,740 m)
Range: 1,200 miles (1,900 km)
Armament: Two nose-mounted machine guns, two wing-mounted cannon, two 500 lb (230 kg) underwing bombs

ASSEMBLY

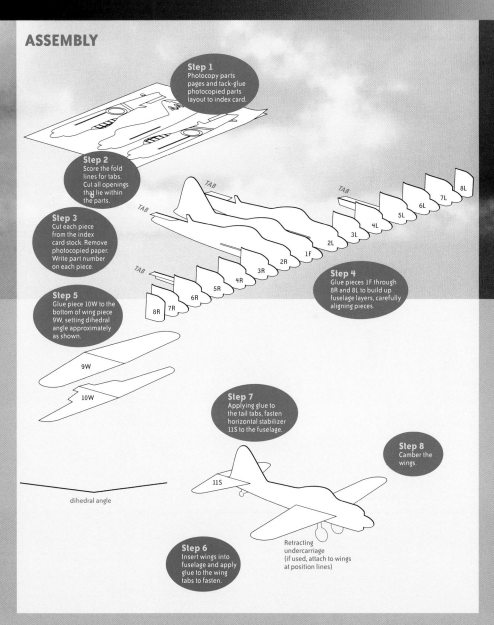

Step 1
Photocopy parts pages and tack-glue photocopied parts layout to index card.

Step 2
Score the fold lines for tabs. Cut all openings that lie within the parts.

Step 3
Cut each piece from the index card stock. Remove photocopied paper. Write part number on each piece.

Step 4
Glue pieces 1F through 8R and 8L to build up fuselage layers, carefully aligning pieces.

Step 5
Glue piece 10W to the bottom of wing piece 9W, setting dihedral angle approximately as shown.

Step 7
Applying glue to the tail tabs, fasten horizontal stabilizer 11S to the fuselage.

Step 8
Camber the wings.

Step 6
Insert wings into fuselage and apply glue to the wing tabs to fasten.

dihedral angle

Retracting undercarriage (if used, attach to wings at position lines)

#11 ILYUSHIN STORMOVIK IL-2

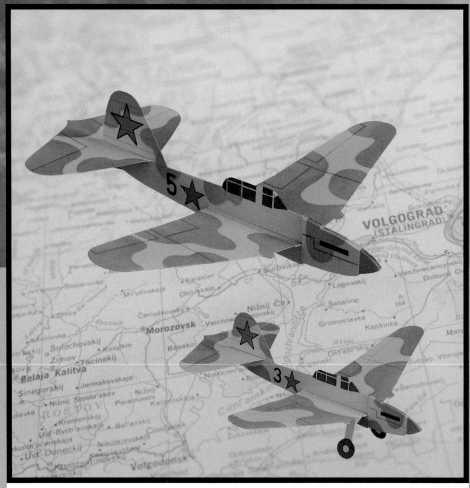

Year: 1941
Country of origin: Russia
Manufacturer: Ilyushin
Type: Two-seat ground attack
Engine: One 1,770 hp inline liquid cooled piston
Wingspan: 48 ft (14.6 m)
Length: 38 ft (11.6 m)
Height: 11 ft 1 in (3.4 m)

Maximum speed: 251 mph (404 km/h)
Service ceiling: 20,000 ft (6,000 m)
Range: 373 miles (600 km)
Armament: Two forward-firing 23 mm cannon,
two forward-firing and rearward-facing
machine guns, and up to 1,321 lb (600 kg)
wing-mounted bombs or rockets

ASSEMBLY

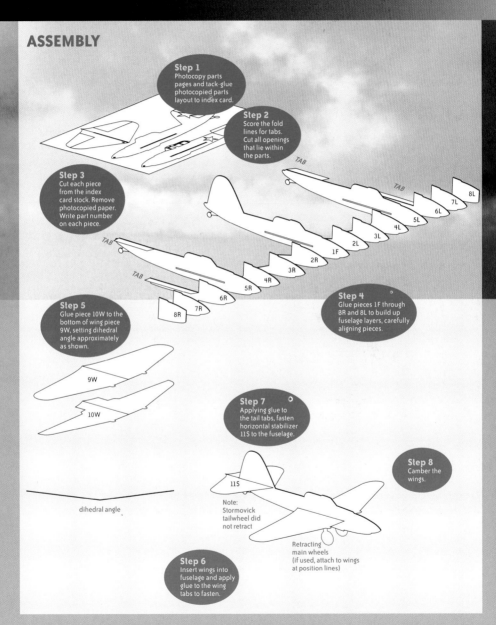

Step 1
Photocopy parts pages and tack-glue photocopied parts layout to index card.

Step 2
Score the fold lines for tabs. Cut all openings that lie within the parts.

Step 3
Cut each piece from the index card stock. Remove photocopied paper. Write part number on each piece.

Step 4
Glue pieces 1F through 8R and 8L to build up fuselage layers, carefully aligning pieces.

Step 5
Glue piece 10W to the bottom of wing piece 9W, setting dihedral angle approximately as shown.

Step 6
Insert wings into fuselage and apply glue to the wing tabs to fasten.

Step 7
Applying glue to the tail tabs, fasten horizontal stabilizer 11S to the fuselage.

Step 8
Camber the wings.

TAB
TAB
TAB
TAB
TAB

8L
7L
6L
5L
4L
3L
2L
1F
2R
3R
4R
5R
6R
7R
8R

9W
10W

dihedral angle

11S

Note: Stormovick tailwheel did not retract

Retracting main wheels (if used, attach to wings at position lines)

33

#12 NORTH AMERICAN P-51 MUSTANG

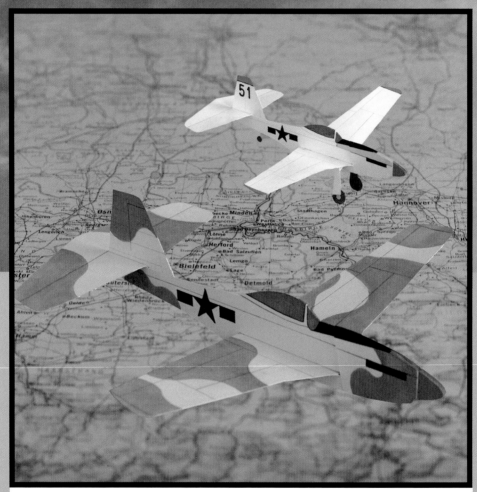

Year: 1942
Country of origin: United States of America
Manufacturer: North American
Type: Single-seat fighter/fighter-bomber
Engine: One 1,490 hp Rolls-Royce Merlin,
12-cylinder, Vee, liquid cooled, supercharger
Wingspan: 37 ft (11.2 m)

Length: 32 ft 3 in (9.9 m)
Height: 12 ft 2 in (3.7 m)
Maximum speed: 437 mph (704 km/h)
Service ceiling: 42,000 ft (12,800 m)
Range: 2,080 miles (3,347 km)
Armament: Six 50 calibre machine-guns,
two external 1,000 lb bombs or six rockets

ASSEMBLY

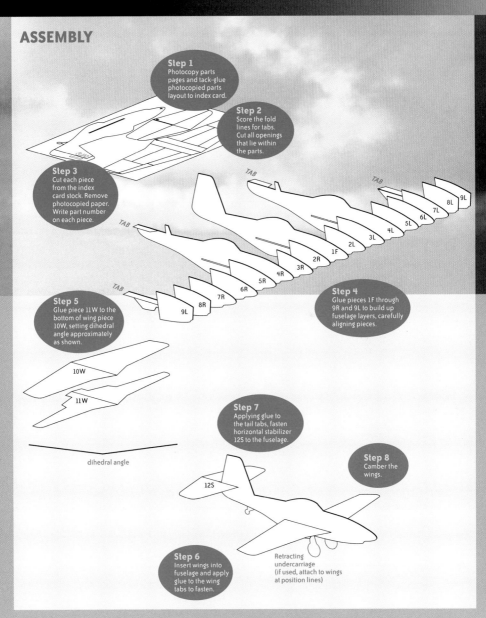

Step 1
Photocopy parts pages and tack-glue photocopied parts layout to index card.

Step 2
Score the fold lines for tabs. Cut all openings that lie within the parts.

Step 3
Cut each piece from the index card stock. Remove photocopied paper. Write part number on each piece.

Step 4
Glue pieces 1F through 9R and 9L to build up fuselage layers, carefully aligning pieces.

Step 5
Glue piece 11W to the bottom of wing piece 10W, setting dihedral angle approximately as shown.

dihedral angle

Step 7
Applying glue to the tail tabs, fasten horizontal stabilizer 12S to the fuselage.

Step 8
Camber the wings.

Step 6
Insert wings into fuselage and apply glue to the wing tabs to fasten.

Retracting undercarriage (if used, attach to wings at position lines)

#13 VOUGHT F4U CORSAIR

Year: 1943
Country of origin: United States of America
Manufacturer: Chance-Vought
Type: Single-seat fighter
Engine: One 2,000 hp Pratt & Whitney air cooled radial piston, supercharger
Wingspan: 41 ft (12.5 m)

Length: 33 ft 4 in (10.2 m)
Height: 16 ft 1 in (4.9 m)
Maximum speed: 417 mph (671 km/h)
Service ceiling: 37,000 ft (11,000 m)
Range: 1,015 miles (1,633 km)
Armament: Six 50 caliber wing-mounted machine guns or four 20 mm cannon

ASSEMBLY

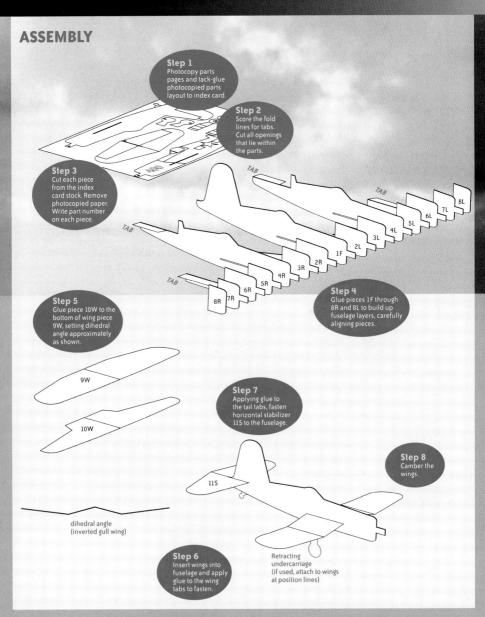

Step 1
Photocopy parts pages and tack-glue photocopied parts layout to index card.

Step 2
Score the fold lines for tabs. Cut all openings that lie within the parts.

Step 3
Cut each piece from the index card stock. Remove photocopied paper. Write part number on each piece.

Step 4
Glue pieces 1F through 8R and 8L to build up fuselage layers, carefully aligning pieces.

Step 5
Glue piece 10W to the bottom of wing piece 9W, setting dihedral angle approximately as shown.

Step 6
Insert wings into fuselage and apply glue to the wing tabs to fasten.

Step 7
Applying glue to the tail tabs, fasten horizontal stabilizer 11S to the fuselage.

Step 8
Camber the wings.

dihedral angle (inverted gull wing)

Retracting undercarriage (if used, attach to wings at position lines)

#14 YAKOVLEV YAK-18

Year: 1943
Country of origin: Russia
Manufacturer: Yakovlev
Type: Two-seat trainer
Engine: One 5-cylinder 145 hp air cooled radial
Wingspan: 33 ft 4 in (10.6 m)

Length: 27 ft 8 in (8.1 m)
Height: 10 ft 7 in (2.7 m)
Maximum speed: 160 mph (250 km/h)
Service ceiling: 17,000 ft (5,100 m)
Range: 450 miles (720 km)
Armament: None or various small bombs

ASSEMBLY

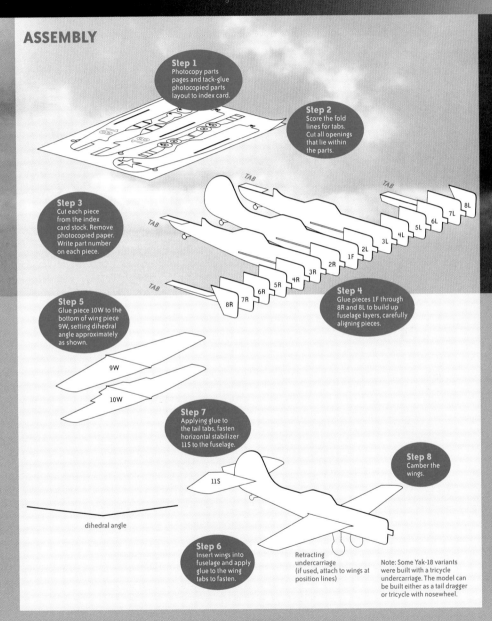

Step 1
Photocopy parts pages and tack-glue photocopied parts layout to index card.

Step 2
Score the fold lines for tabs. Cut all openings that lie within the parts.

Step 3
Cut each piece from the index card stock. Remove photocopied paper. Write part number on each piece.

Step 4
Glue pieces 1F through 8R and 8L to build up fuselage layers, carefully aligning pieces.

Step 5
Glue piece 10W to the bottom of wing piece 9W, setting dihedral angle approximately as shown.

Step 7
Applying glue to the tail tabs, fasten horizontal stabilizer 11S to the fuselage.

Step 8
Camber the wings.

Step 6
Insert wings into fuselage and apply glue to the wing tabs to fasten.

dihedral angle

Retracting undercarriage (if used, attach to wings at position lines)

Note: Some Yak-18 variants were built with a tricycle undercarriage. The model can be built either as a tail dragger or tricycle with nosewheel.

39

#15 MIKOYAN-GUREVICH MIG-15

Year: 1949
Country of origin: Russia
Manufacturer: Mikoyan-Gurevich
Type: Single-seat fighter/fighter-bomber
Engine: One 5,952 lb thrust Klimov
afterburning turbojet
Wingspan: 33 ft (9.9 m)

Length: 35 ft 7 in (10.7 m)
Height: 12 ft 1 in (3.6 m)
Maximum speed: 668 mph (1,070 km/h)
Service ceiling: 50,900 ft (15,270 m)
Range: 1,156 miles (1,849 km)
Armament: One 37 mm and two 23 mm
cannon in the nose, up to 1,100 lb of mixed
underwing bombs and missiles

ASSEMBLY

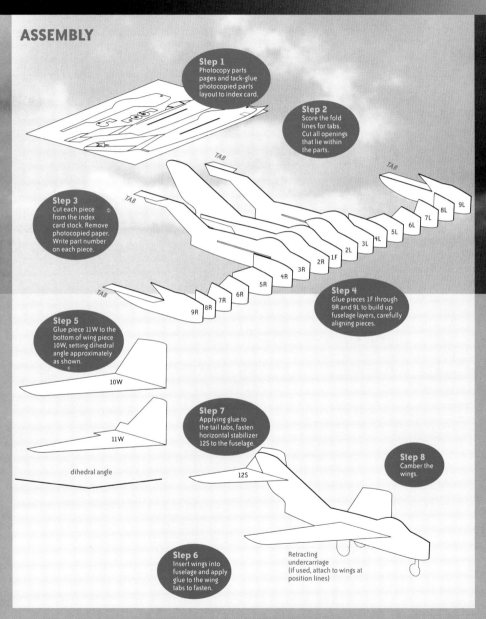

Step 1
Photocopy parts pages and tack-glue photocopied parts layout to index card.

Step 2
Score the fold lines for tabs. Cut all openings that lie within the parts.

Step 3
Cut each piece from the index card stock. Remove photocopied paper. Write part number on each piece.

Step 4
Glue pieces 1F through 9R and 9L to build up fuselage layers, carefully aligning pieces.

Step 5
Glue piece 11W to the bottom of wing piece 10W, setting dihedral angle approximately as shown.

Step 6
Insert wings into fuselage and apply glue to the wing tabs to fasten.

Step 7
Applying glue to the tail tabs, fasten horizontal stabilizer 12S to the fuselage.

Step 8
Camber the wings.

dihedral angle

Retracting undercarriage (if used, attach to wings at position lines)

TAB 10W 11W 12S

41

#16 NORTH AMERICAN F-86 SABRE

Year: 1949
Country of origin: United States of America
Manufacturer: North American
Type: Single-seat fighter/fighter-bomber
Engine: One General Electric J-47 7,500 lb
thrust afterburning turbojet
Wingspan: 39 ft (11.7 m)

Length: 37 ft 6 in (11.3 m)
Height: 14 ft 3 in (4.2 m)
Maximum speed: 678 mph (1,084 km/h)
Service ceiling: 50,000 ft (15,000 m)
Range: 1,200 miles (1,900 km)
Armament: Six 50 calibre machine guns,
two missiles, various external bombs

ASSEMBLY

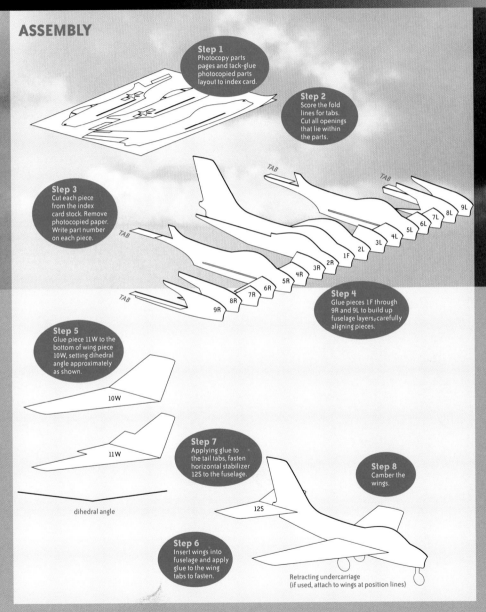

Step 1
Photocopy parts pages and tack-glue photocopied parts layout to index card.

Step 2
Score the fold lines for tabs. Cut all openings that lie within the parts.

Step 3
Cut each piece from the index card stock. Remove photocopied paper. Write part number on each piece.

Step 4
Glue pieces 1F through 9R and 9L to build up fuselage layers, carefully aligning pieces.

Step 5
Glue piece 11W to the bottom of wing piece 10W, setting dihedral angle approximately as shown.

Step 7
Applying glue to the tail tabs, fasten horizontal stabilizer 12S to the fuselage.

Step 8
Camber the wings.

Step 6
Insert wings into fuselage and apply glue to the wing tabs to fasten.

10W

11W

dihedral angle

12S

Retracting undercarriage
(if used, attach to wings at position lines)

TAB

43

#17 MCDONNELL-DOUGLAS F-4 PHANTOM

Year: 1960
Country of origin: United States of America
Manufacturer: McDonnell-Douglas
Type: Single-seat fighter/fighter-bomber
Engine: Two General Electric J79 17,900 lb
thrust afterburning turbojets
Wingspan: 38 ft 5 in (11.5 m)

Length: 63 ft (18.9 m)
Height: 16 ft 6 in (4.9 m)
Maximum speed: 1,485 mph (2,376 km/h)
Service ceiling: 62,000 ft (18,600 m)
Range: 1,100 miles (1,760 km)
Armament: Up to 3,020 lb of cannon, bombs,
or missiles under fuselage and up to 12,500 lb
under the wings

ASSEMBLY

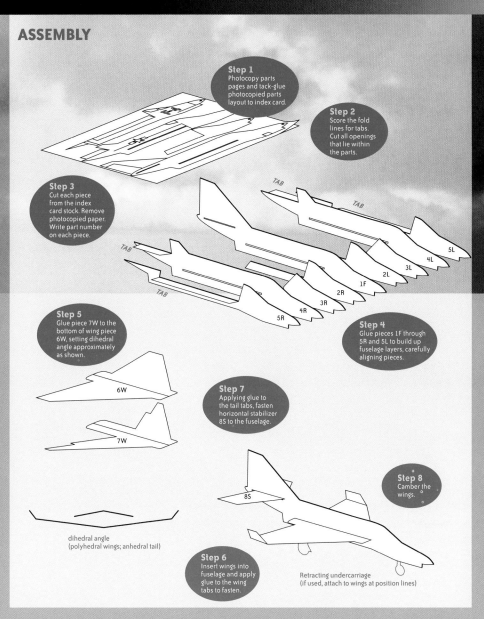

Step 1
Photocopy parts pages and tack-glue photocopied parts layout to index card.

Step 2
Score the fold lines for tabs. Cut all openings that lie within the parts.

Step 3
Cut each piece from the index card stock. Remove photocopied paper. Write part number on each piece.

Step 4
Glue pieces 1F through 5R and 5L to build up fuselage layers, carefully aligning pieces.

Step 5
Glue piece 7W to the bottom of wing piece 6W, setting dihedral angle approximately as shown.

Step 7
Applying glue to the tail tabs, fasten horizontal stabilizer 8S to the fuselage.

Step 8
Camber the wings.

Step 6
Insert wings into fuselage and apply glue to the wing tabs to fasten.

dihedral angle
(polyhedral wings; anhedral tail)

Retracting undercarriage
(if used, attach to wings at position lines)

45

#18 PANAVIA TORNADO

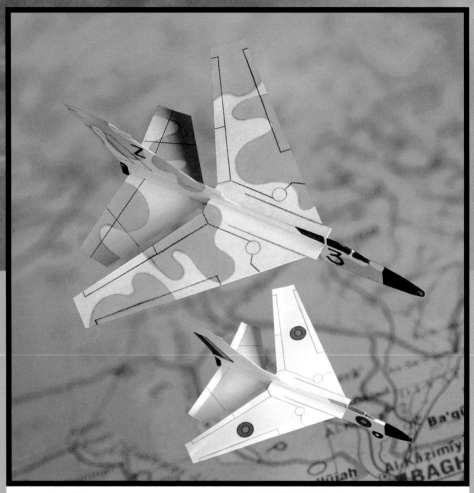

Year: 1980
Country of origin: Britain, Germany, Italy
Manufacturer: Panavia
Type: Two-seat fighter/fighter-bomber
Engine: Two Turbo-Union 14,480 lb thrust
afterburning turbojets
Wingspan: 45 ft 7 in (13.7 m) unswept, 28 ft
2 in (8.4 m) swept

Length: 54 ft 9 in (16.5 m)
Height: 19 ft 6 in (5.9 m)
Maximum speed: 1,452 mph (2,323 km/h)
Service ceiling: 50,000 ft (15,000 m)
Range: 2,432 miles (3,890 km) with 4 drop tanks
Armament: Two 27 mm internal cannon,
up to 20,000 lb (9,000 kg) external missiles
and bombs

ASSEMBLY

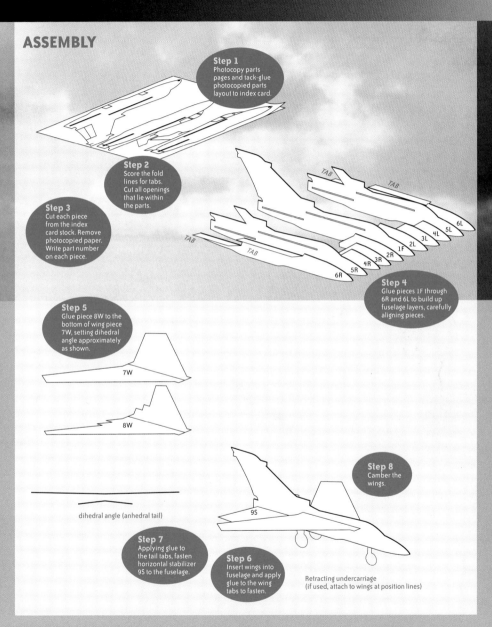

Step 1
Photocopy parts pages and tack-glue photocopied parts layout to index card.

Step 2
Score the fold lines for tabs. Cut all openings that lie within the parts.

Step 3
Cut each piece from the index card stock. Remove photocopied paper. Write part number on each piece.

Step 4
Glue pieces 1F through 6R and 6L to build up fuselage layers, carefully aligning pieces.

Step 5
Glue piece 8W to the bottom of wing piece 7W, setting dihedral angle approximately as shown.

7W

8W

dihedral angle (anhedral tail)

Step 8
Camber the wings.

9S

Step 7
Applying glue to the tail tabs, fasten horizontal stabilizer 9S to the fuselage.

Step 6
Insert wings into fuselage and apply glue to the wing tabs to fasten.

Retracting undercarriage
(if used, attach to wings at position lines)

TAB TAB TAB TAB

5R 4R 3R 2R 1F 1L 2L 3L 4L 5L 6L

6R

INDEX